MAKE IT TODAY FOR Pre-K Play

Written by Joyce Hamman
Edited by Linda Milliken
Design by Wendy Loreen
Illustrated by Barb Lorseyedi & Priscilla Burris
Cover Illustration by Priscilla Burris

Introduction

Movement is natural to young children. It is a way for them to express their creativity and discover their surroundings. Time has shown that a sequential program in motor development activities or movement activities helps young children learn how to use their bodies as effectively as possible. The mastery of various perceptual motor skills enhances the challenges a child will face during the school years. When moving a child can build confidence and express uniqueness in many different ways.

Ask for parent volunteers to help make the equipment detailed in this book. Some require sawing and sanding, tasks which enable Moms and Dads to become involved. Send a letter home detailing equipment materials needed and request for construction help. Schedule afternoon workshops or provide photocopied instructions for home construction.

About the Author

Joyce Hamman has over 16 years experience working with early childhood developmental programs. She is a frequent speaker for the National Association for the Education of Young Children. Joyce currently educates kindergartners at the American School of the Hague, Netherlands. The equipment and program ideas offered here were developed and tested at the Presbyterian Community School, Dana Point, California, Sally Young, Director.

© 1993 **Edupress** • P.O. Box 883 • Dana Point, CA 92629

ISBN 1-56472-014-4

TABLE OF CONTENTS

Testing & Assessment Charts 3

Age Expectations/Definition of Terms 7

MAKE-IT TODAY EQUIPMENT:

1. Whammer Bammers 8

A hand-held, lightweight racket used to develop eye/hand coordination.

2. Tennis Ball Toss-Um 14

A self-contained throwing and catching aid that develops large motor skills.

3. Hoop Loops 20

A pliable plastic hoop develops unilateral movement.

4. Wobble Boards 26

A stand-upon board that moves to increase balance and laterality.

5. Clip-Clop Cans 32

Walking aids that increase body awareness, laterality and coordination.

6. Swishy Streamers 38

Hand-held streamers develop spatial awareness and cross lateral movement.

7. Launching Pads 44

A simple catapult develops eye/hand and eye/foot coordination.

8. Criss-Cross Cones 50

Converted traffic cones build cross lateral movement and kinesthetic senses.

9. Beany Bags 56

Multi-use tactile bags are tools for developing a variety of motor skills.

10. Sit-Down Scooters 62

A rolling board promotes unilateral, bilateral and locomotor movement.

11. Lummi Sticks 68

Rhythm instruments develop the midline, laterality and bilateral movement.

12. Jumping Bean Boxes 74

A "jump-off" platform enhances motor planning and body awareness.

Resources/Books, Tapes, and Records 80

Make it Today for Pre-K Play   © Edupress

Before beginning a perceptual motor development program it is helpful to assess the level of performance your children are capable of. The following screening should be beneficial in finding the strengths and weaknesses of the children you will be working with. It is meant to be only a guiding tool for you when you set up your program each year.

SKILLS CHECKLIST

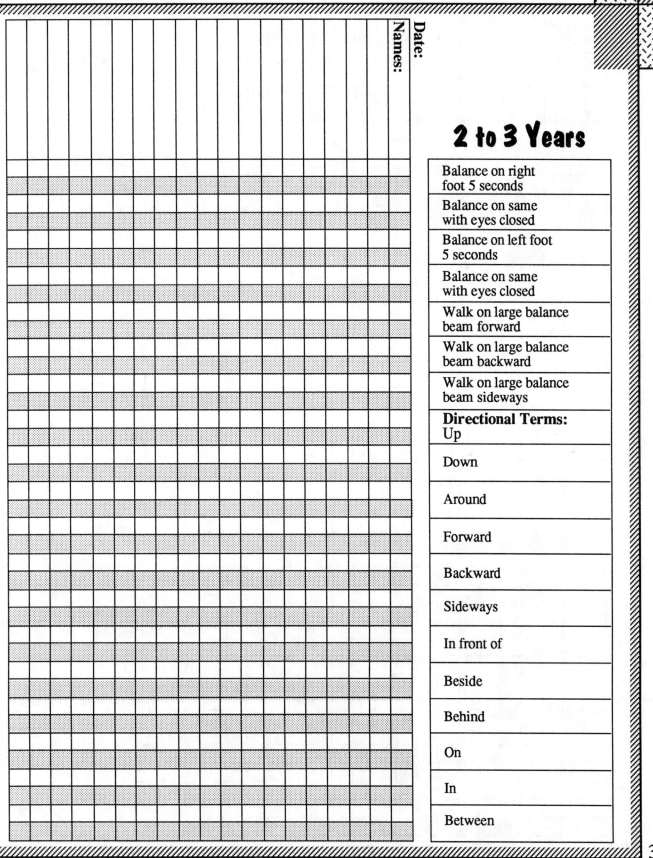

Date:

Names:

2 to 3 Years

Balance on right foot 5 seconds
Balance on same with eyes closed
Balance on left foot 5 seconds
Balance on same with eyes closed
Walk on large balance beam forward
Walk on large balance beam backward
Walk on large balance beam sideways
Directional Terms: Up
Down
Around
Forward
Backward
Sideways
In front of
Beside
Behind
On
In
Between

SKILLS CHECKLIST continued

2 to 3 Years

Date:

	Names:
Across	
Over	
Under	
Nod your head	
Bend your elbows	
Clap your hands	
Open your mouth	
Shrug your shoulders	
Bend your knees	
Stamp your feet	
Jump ten times in a circle	
Jump and land (jump box)	
Throw and catch with partner	
Kick ball to make contact	
Follow a two-direction sequence	
Stork stand for 3 seconds	
Identify: Head	
Ears	
Eyes	
Mouth	
Nose	

Date:

Names:

	Chin
	Neck
	Forehead
	Shoulders
	Chest
	Arm
	Elbow
	Wrist
	Hand
	Fingers
	Waist
	Hip
	Knee
	Ankle
	Heel
	Foot
	Toe
	Side
	Thumb
	Tongue
	Eyebrow

Date:

Names:

	Walk on little balance beam forward
	Walk on little balance beam backward
	Walk on little balance beam sideways
	Walk on little balance beam with bean bag on head
	Crisscross applesauce
	Hop five times on left foot
	Hop five times on right foot
	Skip across room
	Gallop across room
	Use tennis ball for an overhand throw
	Use red ball for underhand throw
	Drop and catch ball
	Throw and catch ball with a partner
	Follow a four-direction sequence
	Logroll
	Kick ball for accuracy
	Jump back and forth across midline
	Heel to toe forward
	Slide step sideways
	Slide step forward
	Slide step backward

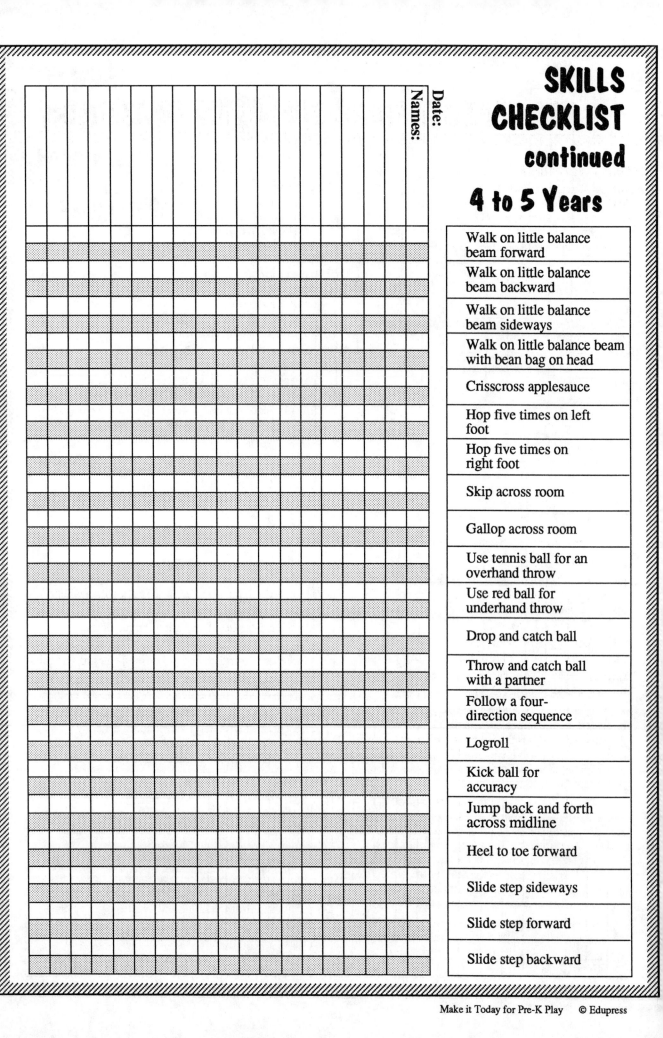

6

AGE EXPECTATIONS/DEFINITION OF TERMS

Age Expectations

Eighteen Months to Two Years
Walks backwards
Walks upstairs with help
Climbs
Begins to understand depth
Dances to music
Begins to identify body parts
Walks on inclines

Two and One-half Years
Kicks ball forward, does not have leg back swing
Jumps in place
Runs (stiffly)
Throws small ball overhand
Pedals tricycle

Three Years
Walks up and down stairs without adult, but usually not alternating feet
Walks a few steps on tiptoe
Jumps up, feet together
Jumps from one step, feet together
Walks backward a short distance
Balances on one foot briefly
Catches with stiff arms

Four Years
Hops on preferred foot
Walks up and down stairs usually alternating feet
Throws ball with precision
Balances on toes
Balances with eyes closed
Jumps over rope or obstacle
Pumps swing
Turns corners quickly
Starts and stops running movements at will
Controls bouncing ball with two hands

Five Years
Hops on either foot
Controls bouncing ball with one hand
Balances on one foot for fifteen seconds
Jumps over obstacles at knee height with feet together
Walks heel to toe forward and backward
Walks on 2x4 balance beam without falling off
Good climbing ability
Skips, gallops and jumps with confidence
Kicks with back swing and control
Marches or dances to music rhythms
Rolls body at different speeds

Definition of Terms

Gross Motor Development: The development and awareness of large muscle activity in the body. The quality of movement increases with and is dependent on developmental age.

Motor Planning: Ability to perceive movement then organize the body to achieve that movement.

Communication Skills: Motor based skills involving reading, writing and speaking.

Body Image or Body Awareness: A concept of one's body and the movements it can make. Awareness of the structure and position of their body parts. Good body awareness provides a solid foundation for developing perceptual motor activities which are necessary for all future learning.

Laterality: Ability to use both sides of the body independently. Awareness of a left side and a right side. Without laterality a child will have trouble with balance, learning how to read, reversing images. (example: If trying to copy someone while looking at them will do motion or movement on the same side rather than reversing.) Laterality is usually and unconscious awareness of movement.

Directionality: A conscious awareness of where things are in relationship to the body. A child needs to be comfortable in laterality before directionality develops.

Unilateral Movements: Movement using only one side of the body. Example: Throw the ball with one hand.)

Bilateral Movements: Movement such as jumping that uses both sides of the body at the same time.

Locomotor Skills: Moving the body from one destination to another. Examples: Jump, hop, skip, gallop, and run.

Spatial Awareness: Awareness of where one's body is in space in relationship to items surrounding the body.

Tactile awareness: The sense of feeling one gets from direct contact with items surrounding the body.

Vestibular System: Sensory receptors in the inner ear which give one their sense of balance.

Kinesthetic Senses: Muscle sense within the body that tells body parts to move. Example: Bend elbow

Eye/Hand Coordination: The ability to use the eyes and hands together to accomplish a skill.

Eye/Foot Coordination: The ability to use the eyes and feet together to accomplish a skill.

Cross Lateral Movements: The ability to use both sides of the body at once. Different body parts compliment each other. Example: Throwing a ball with one hand and balancing weight on the opposite foot.

Midline: The ability to place a body part across an imaginary line running down the middle of the body. Example: Place right foot over and beside the left foot.

1

WHAMMER BAMMERS

Materials Needed to Make One Whammer Bammer:

- One wire coat hanger
- One nylon stocking
- Electrical tape or plastic tape (several different colors if making more than one racket)
- Scissors

"A Whammer Bammer is a hand-held, lightweight racket used to develop hand-eye coordination."

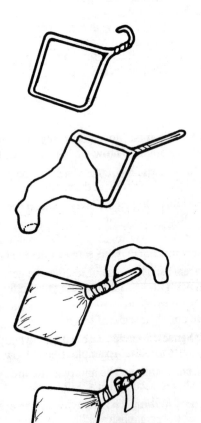

Assembling Directions:

1. Hold the hanger hook in one hand. With the other hand, stretch the hanger body into a diamond shape.

2. Straighten the hanger hook.

3. Starting at the tip of the triangle opposite the handle, slide the hanger into the nylon stocking.

4. Pull the stocking tightly over the hanger. Wrap the excess around the handle.

5. Wrap plastic or masking tape around the handle. Use enough tape to hold the stocking in place, cover sharp edges and add bulk to make gripping by small hands easier.

Motor Development Skills

- Spatial Awareness
- Laterality
- Directionality
- Eye/Hand Coordination
- Body Awareness

Safety Rules

- Never hit anyone with the racket.
- Do not put the racket in your mouth.
- Do not put a balloon in your mouth.
- Never chase after a balloon, ball or other object hit outside the supervised playing area.

Teaching Tips

※ Discuss the safety rules prior to using the equipment.

※ *Whammer Bammer* activities are best accomplished indoors. If using the equipment outdoors, choose a day that is not windy.

※ Popping balloons may startle the children. Demonstrate the sound in advance and caution them against overreacting. Playing indoors will decrease these occurrences.

※ Incorporate laterality and directionality terms—up, down, over, left, right—into students' play with the *Whammer Bammer*.

※ Allow plenty of space so that each child has room to freely move the *Whammer Bammer* without hitting another child. If space is limited, work with smaller groups. Involve children awaiting their turns in counting and retrieving activities.

WHAMMER BAMMERS

Getting Started

Before giving the children a *Whammer Bammer,* have them swing their arms

- from side-to-side
- along the side of their bodies from back to front
- from the floor towards the ceiling

Once children are comfortable with these movements put the *Whammer Bammer* handle in the palm of their hand. Position their hand so the *Whammer Bammer* is horizontal to the floor. Practice moving the paddle from the floor to the ceiling several times. This is the most successful movement when they begin interaction with a balloon because the balloon will usually return to the child close to the point of contact.

As children begin to master the basic "up" motion of hitting with the *Whammer Bammer* they will be ready to "swoosh" the paddle in a vertical position from side to side. Older children may try to swing the paddle along the side of the body from back to front as if completing an "underhand serve".

Now you are ready to add another element. Blow up a nine-inch (22 cm) balloon for each child. Practice striking the balloon with the *Whammer Bammer* toward the ceiling. Remind children of the correct upward movement. As children gain confidence ask them to count the number of times they strike the balloon.

For a further challenge, replace balloons with various sized foam balls. Control the height of the ball's loft by increasing and decreasing the size of the swing. Children will begin to draw their own conclusions as to the differences in the results.

Make it Today for Pre-K Play   © Edupress

Further Activities

Partner: appropriate for the four- and five-year old child.

Pick a partner and stand facing each other about six feet apart. Use the *Whammer Bammer* like a tennis racket. Swing the racket along the side of the body from back to front. Try to hit the balloon to the partner. As confidence is gained, the space between partners can be increased. Partners can count the number of successive hits or time the length the balloon "rally" can be kept going.

For a greater challenge, use masking tape to mark the boundaries of a playing court. Add a rope or net over which to hit the balloon or foam ball. Hang colorful scarves from the rope to make it easier for the children judge if they hit the ball over rather than under the rope.

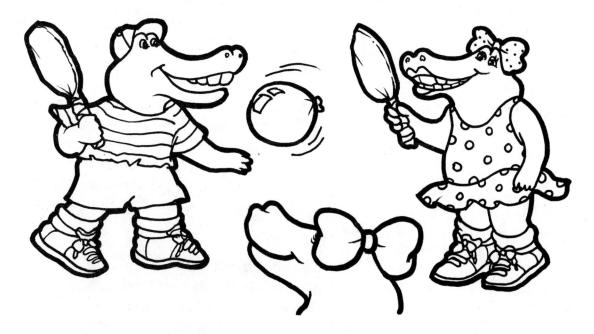

Group: *appropriate for the four- and five-year old child.*

Arrange children in a circle, spacing far enough apart to move the *Whammer Bammer* freely. Hit the balloon around the circle in a clockwise movement. Hit the balloon across the circle trying to make a predetermined number of hits.

WHAMMER BAMMERS

More Movement

Music

Movin', a Hap Palmer recording, (see Resources, page 80), has several instrumental songs of varying tempos the children can move to while using their *Whammer Bammers*. Try swinging up and down then from side to side in time to the music.

Chants

Listen to the words and move the *Whammer Bammer*.

> *Wam, wam, bam, bam.*
> *Whammer Bammer we've had fun today.*
> *We've worked our legs, we've worked our arms*
> *Now it's time for restful play*

> *Swish, swoosh, swish, swoosh.*
> *Feel the wind my Whammer Bammer*
> *   makes on my face.*
> *It taps my balloon and sends it on a*
> *   journey,*
> *Sailing into outer space.*

Game

Play a shape game with the *Whammer Bammers*. Pin a shape—triangle, square, circle or rectangle—to each child's shirt. Stand in a circle. Spread far enough apart so that everyone has room to swing the racket. Play the game with the squares hitting only to the squares. Continue play until all shapes have had a turn.

Curriculum Integration

Science

Study air and wind. Talk about what is in a balloon. Blow one up in front of the children and ask them to describe what they saw happen.

Compare the height of the balloon's loft when struck with a fast swing and a slow swing of the *Whammer Bammer*.

Ask children to fan themselves with their *Whammer Bammer*. What do they feel on their face? Fan a friend. Fan fast. Fan slowly. Try to move a lightweight object by fanning it.

Connect with literature:

> ***Millicent and the Wind*** by Robert Munsch; Annick Press, 1984. The wind surprises a young girl with friendship.

> ***Mirandy and Brother Wind*** by The Trumpet Club, 1988. A little girl has many adventures as she tries to catch "brother wind".

Snack

Make a *Whammer Bammer* for snack. Turn a slice of cheese so children can see the diamond shape. Add a pretzel handle on one point of the cheese. Set a "balloon" grape on top. Enjoy!

Art

Construct several extra *Whammer Bammers* to use at an art center. Cut a cardboard pattern. Lay the pattern on top of a piece of construction paper. Hold the *Whammer Bammer* above the stencil. Brush paint on the *Whammer Bammer*. The paint should splatter onto the stencil. Remove the stencil. The design will appear on the construction paper.

TENNIS BALL TOSS-UM

2

Materials Needed to Make One Tennis Ball Toss-Um:

- One empty gallon bleach container with built-in handle
- 36" (1 meter) clothesline rope
- Tennis ball
- Scissors
- Ice pick (or hammer and nail)

"A Tennis Ball Toss-Um is a self-contained throwing and catching aid that develops large motor skills."

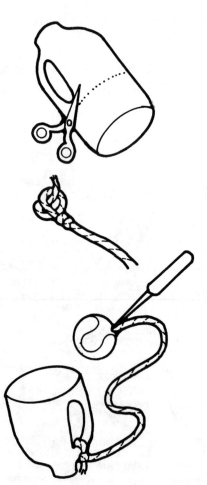

Assembling Directions:

1. Thoroughly wash and dry the empty bleach container.

2. Cut the bleach bottle in half across the width approximately one inch (2.54 cm) above the handle.

3. Tie several knots at one end of the clothesline.

4. Carefully push the knotted end of the line through the middle of the tennis ball with the ice pick. Do not come out the other side. The knot should be "hidden" inside the ball.

5. Tie the other end of the clothesline with a secure knot to the handle of the container.

TENNIS BALL TOSS-UM

Motor Development Skills

- Eye/Hand Coordination
- Unilateral Movement
- Directionality
- Motor Planning

Safety Rules

- Always stand still when using the *Tennis Ball Toss-Um.*
- Hold the *Tennis Ball Toss-Um* only by the handle. Do not hold the ball to swing it around.
- Swing the ball slowly to keep the rope from wrapping around a body part.

Teaching Tips

✎ Discuss the safety rules prior to using the equipment..

✎ *Tennis Ball Toss-Um* activities can be done anywhere that allows enough space for each child to swing their rope and not hit a neighbor.

✎ This equipment is most appropriate for the four- and five-year-old child. They will have the most success if *Whammer Bammers* have already been introduced.

✎ The *Tennis Ball Toss-Um* is a piece of equipment that children need to experience over and over again for mastery. Caution them in advance not to become frustrated with slow progress..

✎ If the rope should get wound around the neck, arm or other body part, instruct children to ask for help unwinding the string and freeing themselves.

TENNIS BALL TOSS-UM

Getting Started

Before giving children the *Tennis Ball Toss-Um,* show them how much space they will need around them so as not to hit anyone with the tennis ball.

Begin by having the children grip the handle of the plastic container so that the opening to the container is pointing up to the ceiling. Start by swinging the ball on the string from the back of the body to the front, along the side of their body.

Once they have mastered the swing, help them to feel the point when they should give an extra "swoop" to propel the ball into the scoop. They may need someone to hold the *Tennis Ball Toss-Um* along with them the first few times. This step is difficult for the children at first but once they find the right spot at which to propel the ball they become very confident. Give this portion of the learning process a great deal of supervision and time.

After some degree of success has been achieved on one side of the body, encourage children to change hands and repeat the learning steps on the other side of their body. Try moving the *Tennis Ball Toss-Um* in front of the body and experiment with the movement at the location. Then try using the *Tennis Ball Toss-Um* in a sitting or standing position.

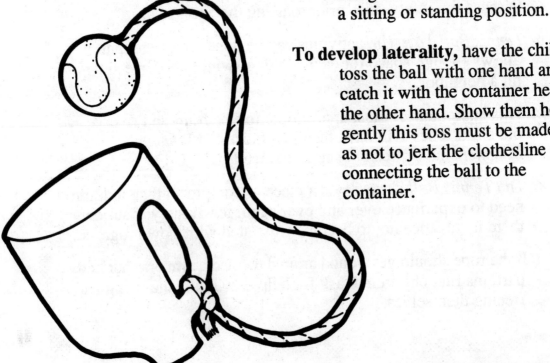

To develop laterality, have the children toss the ball with one hand and catch it with the container held in the other hand. Show them how gently this toss must be made so as not to jerk the clothesline connecting the ball to the container.

Further Activities

Station Play:

Set up several *Tennis Ball Toss-Um* stations around the playground. Allow plenty of room between them. At each station, put a picture clue that illustrates how the child is to use the *Tennis Ball Toss-Um* at that particular station. One may be standing, one sitting, one in the right hand, one in the left hand.

Signal children with a predetermined sound or action when it is time to move to the next station. To facilitate movement between stations, call out a particular action such as tiptoeing, walking backwards or crawling.

When it is time to cool-down and close up the stations, invite the children to help by "putting the turtle to sleep" under its shell. That means to put the ball carefully in the scoop without tangling the clothesline.

TENNIS BALL TOSS-UM

More Movement

Music   (See Resources, page 80.)

The Slow, Fast, Soft, Loud Clap Song, from **Songs About Me** helps children get
the feeling of the fast and slow movements needed to propel the ball. Also
on the same album, *I'm Swaying My Body* helps the children learn to
swing their arms for proper use of the *Tennis Ball Toss-Um.*

Chants

Listen to the words and move the *Tennis Ball Toss-Um.*

> *Toss-um, Toss-um in the air.*
> *Where you Toss-um, we don't care.*
> *Toss-um high. Toss-um low.*
> *Toss-um, toss-um wherever you go.*

Say this chant while putting away the *Tennis Ball Toss-Um*

> *Slowly, slowly, Mr. Turtle moves.*
> *Down the road to take a snooze!*
> *Now he is rested and ready for fun.*
> *Slowly, slowly in the bright sun!*

Game

Play an observation game with three *Tennis Ball Toss-Ums.* Add an extra
ball to one. Turn them all upside-down so the balls are hidden inside.
Show children which container has two balls hidden in it. Tell them to
watch carefully as you change the positions of the containers by
sliding them along a tabletop. Ask children to identify the container
they think has the two balls in it.

TENNIS BALL TOSS-UM

Curriculum Integration

Science

Turn the *Tennis Ball Toss-Um* upside-down and swing the ball back and forth like a pendulum. Teach the children the movement. Line up several small items such as corks, empty film cannisters and small foam balls on the floor. Carefully swing the *Tennis Ball Toss-Um* pendulum . so that you hit the different items. What happens to the different items as they are hit? Does the size or weight of the item make a difference? The children can experiment in pairs with other objects . Be sure there is enough space between working pairs so that no one gets struck by a swinging pendulum!

Snack

Make turtles—but not the candy kind! Let the children try to crack walnuts. (Save the shells for art.) Cover the nut meat with peanut butter. Roll the peanut butter walnut in crushed pretzels. Stick on four raisin feet and a grape head.

Art

Use the walnut shell leftover from snack to make a miniature turtle. Fingerpaint the shell green. Glue on a button head.

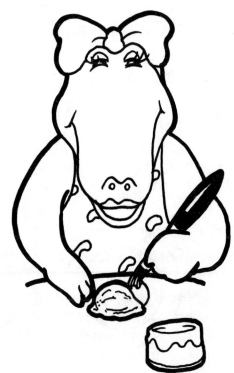

Craft

Make a mini Toss-Um to take home. Use a plastic cup, a yard (meter) of string and a large pom-pom. Tie the pom-pom to one end of the string. Poke the other end of the string through the bottom of the cup. Tie a knot to hold the string in place.

3 HOOP LOOPS

Materials Needed to Make One Hoop Loop:

- 3 feet (1 meter) pliable plastic tubing 1/2" to 3/4" (1.25 cm) diameter
- Sturdy scissors • White glue
- Small handsaw or clippers
- 1 1/2"(4 cm)-wide plastic tape in various colors
- Wooden dowel (sized to fit inside plastic tubing)

"A Hoop Loop is a light weight plastic circle that fits completely over the body."

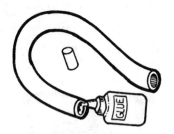

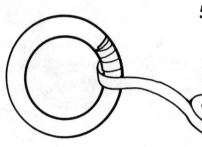

Assembling Directions:

1. Cut the wooden dowel into 1 1/2 inch (4 cm) lengths.

2. Place a small amount of white glue inside each end of the plastic tubing.

3. Insert the wooden dowel into one glued end of the plastic tubing.

4. Slide the other end of the plastic tubing over the dowel to form a circle.

5. Wrap plastic tape around the tube to reinforce the closing. Use various colors of tape for color sorting and categorizing in later use of the equipment.

Make it Today for Pre-K Play   © Edupress

Motor Development Skills

- Midline
- Laterality
- Directionality
- Gross Motor Development
- Motor Planning

Safety Rules

- Never throw a *Hoop Loop*.
- Never pull a friend around with a *Hoop Loop*.
- Do not tug on the area by the dowel. Doing so may cause the *Hoop Loop* to come apart.

Teaching Tips

※ *Hoop Loop*s are appropriate for all ages.

※ Be sure to make enough *Hoop Loops* so all the children in the group can have one of their own to use.

※ When determining the diameter of the *Hoop Loops*, take into account the size of the children. Be sure the *Hoop Loops* will fit over their bodies as well as being large enough to enable them to jump from one *Hoop Loop* to another.

※ You can make a storage rack for a *Hoop Loop* by carving a groove across the width of a wooden block. Sand the block to a smooth finish. Stand the *Hoop Loop* upright in the groove. Children can also move around and through the *Hoop Loop* in this upright position.

HOOP LOOPS

Getting Started

Before beginning any activities, give children a chance to "get acquainted" with the *Hoop Loop*. Hold it in one hand and then in two. Put the hands together on the *Hoop Loop*. Now move them to opposite sides. Set the *Hoop Loop* on the ground and step inside. Now try jumping inside. Grasp the *Hoop Loop* again while still standing inside, and move it up the body and over the head.

Start by using the *Hoop Loop* to develop directionality and spatial awareness. Give each child a hoop and have them follow your verbal directions. "Place the *Hoop Loop* beside your body." "Hold the *Hoop Loop* over your head." "Stand inside your *Hoop Loop*." "Set your *Hoop Loop* on the ground and walk around it."

Put all the *Hoop Loops* on the ground in a straight line to develop laterality and bilaterality. Jump through the *Hoop Loops* in sequence. Now try hopping through them. Make a more difficult path for older children by placing the *Hoop Loops* in a curve or putting two side-by-side.

The *Hoop Loops* can also be used for developing unilateral skills by having the child throw a bean bag into a *Hoop Loop*. The child should stand on a carpet remnant approximately three to six feet (one to three meters) away depending on their age and skill level. Younger children should begin by using an underhand throw.

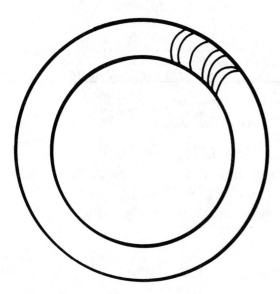

A further challenge for older children would be to throw the bean bags into the *Hoop Loops* in a specific order. Numbers could be placed into the *Hoop Loops* to indicate this order. Verbal directions could incorporate words such as first, second and third.

Make it Today for Pre-K Play   © Edupress

Further Activities

Obstacle Course:

Set up an obstacle course for the four- and five-year-old children using the *Hoop Loops*. Children can move through the course hopping, crawling, skipping, walking forwards and backwards, bouncing a ball or throwing a bean bag. Vary the difficulty of the course according to match and challenge children's capabilities.

Younger children are capable of jumping through a course of three to four hoops. They also enjoy crawling over and through the hoops.

When it's time to clean up the obstacle course invite the children to help you gather the hoops by placing them on their wrist, around their necks, or over their shoulders.

Eventually children will be able to get involved in setting up the course. They can incorporate the actions with which they are familiar. They may also be encouraged to create some new, innovative uses with the *Hoop Loops*.

HOOP LOOPS

More Movement

Music   (See Resources, page 80).

Learning With Circles and Sticks by Hap Palmer

• *Circles Everywhere* provides the opportunity to use the *Hoop Loops* in a variety of quiet and relaxing ways.

• *Jump and Land* actively reinforces directionality.

You'll need lots of room, outdoors or in, to hear *Rockabilly Whoa!* from ***Learning Through Movement and Song, Volume I*** by Sheri Senter. Place the *Hoop Loops* all around the area. Start the music and encourage children to move creatively in time to the music. When the music stops, the child must find a *Hoop Loop* and respond in a predetermined way such as to sit in it, put one foot inside and one out or stand inside on one foot.

Chants

> *Jump and land as fast as you can,*
> *Be sure your feet touch whenever you land.*
> *Quickly now, jump up high,*
> *See if you can touch the sky!*

> *You have jumped and you have crawled*
> *From one circle to the next*
> *And now your body is ready for a rest.*
> *Come and join me now in our group,*
> *And let's hope that we are all not too pooped,*
> *To sing a song or play a quiet game,*
> *Or maybe even pretend we are circling in a plane!*

Game

Place two *Hoop Loops* on the floor. Fill one with yellow items and the other with blue by choosing children to find something in the room of either color. When the *Hoop Loops* are filled, return the items to their original locations. Play the game again using two different colors. For older children, decide on a category rather than a color for each *Hoop Loop*. Ask the children to fill the hoops with items fitting that category. Examples: Things that "go" or things made of metal.

Curriculum Integration

Literature

Shape books which incorporate the circular shape of *Hoops Loops* are
appropriate for curriculum integration.
> ***Round & Round & Round*** by Tana Hoban; Greenwillow Books 1983.
> A color photographic book featuring things that are round.
> ***If You Give A Mouse A Cookie*** by Laura Jaffe Numeroff; Harper and
> Row 1985. A mouse is given a cookie then gets carried away.

Snack

Have a circular-shape snack. Slice bananas, carrots and cucumbers. Compare
color, size and texture of the different foods.

Art

Make paint prints on colorful construction paper with a variety of circular-
shaped items. Give the children tempera paint in which to dip the
items. A few examples are canisters, lids, corks and various diameters
of PVC pipe.

Math

Increase children's knowledge of
size discrimination and
comparison.

Provide children with a *Hoop Loop*.
Ask them to find things they
think the Hoop Loop will fit
over. Have them walk around
and test their thoughts.

Thinking creatively, try to imagine
and name things the *Hoop
Loops* would and wouldn't fit
over that are not presently
within sight. Would it fit over
an elephant? An ant?

WOBBLE BOARDS

Materials Needed to Make One Wobble Board:

- 7/8" (2.54 cm) Plywood
- 1" x 1" x 12" (2.54 x 2.54 x 30 cm) length of wood
- Small nails   • Sandpaper
- Hammer
- Circular saw, hand saw
- Enamel paint and brush
- Permanent marker

"A Wobble Board is a rocking board that can be manipulated side to side to develop balance and laterality."

Assembling Directions:

1. Cut the plywood into a one-foot (30 cm) square.

2. Use the hand saw to cut the 1" x 1" length of wood into a one-foot (30 cm) length, if not already cut to this size.

3. Sand the edges of both pieces of wood until smooth to touch.

4. Nail the one-foot length of wood across the center of the plywood square. Be sure the nails do not go through to the other side.

5. Paint the boards a bright color (optional). Whether you paint them or not use a permanent marker to trace footprints onto the top of the board so the child knows how to position themselves on the equipment. (Toes should be pointing out slightly to the side.)

26

WOBBLE BOARDS

Motor Development Skills

- Laterality
- Body Balance

Safety Rules

- It is important to stand on the board correctly to avoid injury.
- Always be standing up near a *Wobble Board* in use in order to avoid pinched fingers.
- Shoes should always be worn in the *Wobble Board* area.
- Never run to or jump onto a *Wobble Board*.

Teaching Tips

- *Wobble Boards* are appropriate for all ages.

- Be sure to review the safety rules, especially with the younger children. Show them how fingers and toes can easily get pinched if they sit or kneel instead of stand on the *Wobble Board*.

- Designate a *Wobble Board* use area.

- It may be helpful to supply each *Wobble Board* user with a low-pile carpet remnant. This can be the area on which to place and use the *Wobble Board*. Other children are not to get fingers or toes near the carpet remnant.

- Find a crate or carton with side openings or handles for easy carrying. Stack the *Wobble Boards* on top of each other rather than on their sides to eliminate the problem of knocking off the nailed-on length of wood.

WOBBLE BOARDS

Getting Started

Before attempting to stand on the *Wobble Board* practice the movement on the ground. First position the children's feet a little bit apart with toes pointed slightly outward. Practice a side-to-side, rocking movement. Do this with legs straight then with knees bent.

Talk about balance. Demonstrate with a bean bag on the head. Show how the movement of the head can cause the bean bag to fall. Together, practice keeping the head straight and still while standing in the *Wobble Board* position and rocking side-to-side.

Place the *Wobble Boards* in an area set off by themselves. Explain to the children that best balance and leverage is obtained by pointing their toes out slightly to the side as they practice earlier. Step onto the *Wobble Board*. Encourage them to match their own feet to the ones that are marked on the top side of the *Wobble Board*.

Allow time for the children to try out the *Wobble Board* until they can discover the best way for them to achieve balance. Encourage them to try different movement speeds while still maintaining balance.

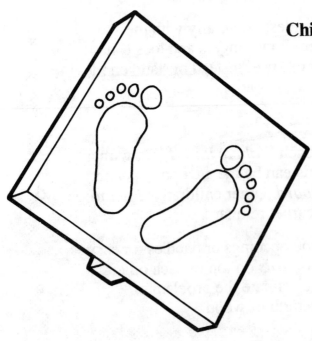

Children may work with another child or an adult when first learning to balance on the *Wobble Board*. Have the partner stand slightly in front and hold hands with the *Wobble Board* user. This will lend a feeling of stability.

Gradually lessen the hold until fingertips are barely touching. When comfortable, the child on the *Wobble Board* may release the partner's hands completely.

Make it Today for Pre-K Play   © Edupress

Further Activities

Once the children are confident on the *Wobble Boards* let them try to place their feet differently to see if the *Wobble Boards* still move in the same way. Are they still able to keep their balance?

Encourage older children to shift their weight as they move their *Wobble Boards*. Are they able to make their *Wobble Boards* move around in a circle by the way they continue to shift and distribute their weight?

Have the older child place a bean bag on their head. Are they able to keep the bean bag on their head while moving the *Wobble Board*? Let them continue to experiment by placing the bean bag on a shoulder, shoe top or other body part.

Younger children can do similar activity by holding the bean bag under the chin, in the palm of their hand or with two hands.

WOBBLE BOARDS

More Movement

Music   (See Resources, page 80.)

There are several good songs to help children develop body balance.

Me and My Bean Bag, by the Learning Station has a song, *Bean Bag Balance*, to accompany bean bag and *Wobble Board* activities. Each child would need a bean bag.

Easy Does It by Hap Palmer has several good songs for *Wobble Board* fun. Try *The Beanbag, Birds in Circles* and *High Wire Artist*.

Bean Bag Activities & Coordination Skills by Georgiana Liccione Stewart has a fun balance-developing song, *Bean Bag Parade*.

Chants

> *Wiggle wobble to and fro,*
> *I hope my balance will not go.*
> *For I might fall into a great big heap,*
> *And that will surely make me weep!*

> *Lean to the left, lean to the right,*
> *Don't let your balance move out of sight.*
> *For if you lose it, down you'll land,*
> *On your knees or maybe a hand.*

Creative Movement

Pretend the *Wobble Board* is a row boat. Encourage the children to think of different ways to move their upper bodies to row their boats. Sing *Row, Row, Row Your Boat* as you are doing the activity.

Older children might enjoy making up their own stories as you do this activity.

WOBBLE BOARDS

Curriculum Integration

Literature

Caps for Sale by Esphyr Slobodkina, Scholastic Book Series, 1940. A hat salesman balances his hats on his head while trying to show off what caps he has for sale. After reading the story, try placing a stack of hats on the head while maneuvering the *Wobble Board!*

Snack

Make your own *Wobble Board* to munch on! Start with a graham cracker square and one pretzel stick. Attach the pretzel to the cracker across the center using the peanut butter as "glue". Give children a few raisins with which to experiment weighing and balancing on their edible *Wobble Board* before eating!

Math

Place a balance scale in the room. Let the children put various items from around the room on the scale to see what will balance or what will make the scale move up and down like a *Wobble Board*. Use the same items and place them on the *Wobble Board* to see if you get the same results.

Art

Paint a wobbly picture. Place a *Wobble Board* in front of a paint easel. Instruct children they are to paint a picture while moving on their *Wobble Board*. Have them compare the different kinds of strokes they get from their paint brushes as a result of the movement.

CLIP CLOP CANS

Materials Needed to Make One Pair of Clip Clop Cans:

- Two empty and cleaned 2.7 pound coffee cans with plastic lids
- Nylon rope (weight used for clothesline)
- Ice pick
- Matches

"Clip Clop Cans are walking aids that increase body awarenesss, laterality and hand, foot coordination."

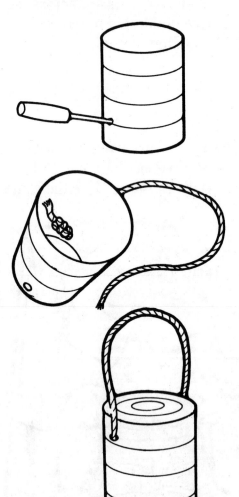

Assembling Directions:

1. Remove the plastic lids. Set the open end of each can on a flat surface.

2. Use the ice pick to make a hole on opposite sides of the can, about one inch (2.54 cm) from the top of the sealed end.

3. Cut two pieces of rope that when attached to the can are long enough for children to comfortably hold yet provide leverage and support when walking. Vary the lengths to accommodate student height.

4. Thread each rope end through a hole. Tie several knots in the ends so the rope will not pull through the hole. Repeat with the second can.

5. Cut off excess rope and use a match to melt the ends to avoid unraveling. Replace the lid over the open end.

Make it Today for Pre-K Play   © Edupress

Motor Development Skills

- Laterality
- Body Awareness
- Eye-Foot Coordination
- Cross-Lateral Movement
- Kinesthetic Sense

Safety Rules

- Keep the plastic lid on the bottom of the can for traction. Replace the plastic lids if they wear out.
- Never attempt to run when on the *Clip Clop Cans*. They are for walking!
- Sturdy shoes should always be worn when using the *Clip Clop Cans*.

Teaching Tips

- *Clip Clop Cans* are a wonderful way to increase a child's ability to balance and move.

- Introduce *Clip Clop Cans* after the child has had a lot of exposure to the balance beam or other balancing activities.

- Always be alert to a child's fear of height when using the *Clip Clop Cans*.

- If children fall off their *Clip Clop Cans* they should know to let the string go so their hands are free to catch themselves if necessary. They should also try to move away from the cans.

- Younger children should always have an adult with them when making their first attempts at walking.

- Periodically check the knots for tightness inside each *Clip Clop Can*.

CLIP CLOP CANS

Getting Started

Clip Clop Cans **should** be introduced after a child has had many experiences on the balance beam, jump box and wobble boards. Younger children should move along slowly at their own pace with an adult nearby.

To introduce this equipment, work with each child alone to be sure they are comfortable and feel safe on top of the cans. Encourage them to point their toes slightly outward to help maintain balance. Practice standing in place, rope in hand, feet pointed outward. After balance has been achieved, practice taking a step forward with each foot.

Before the child takes additional steps, be sure they understand what to do should they fall off the *Clip Clop Cans*. Practice some "falls". Let go of the rope and try to move out of the way of the cans. Then practice getting back on the *Clip Clop Cans* and getting repositioned, rope in hand, feet pointed outward.

As their confidence builds let the children move about freely around the room or designated use area. Remind them to hold onto their ropes tightly to help maintain their balance. A path should be set up so all the children are moving in the same direction.

Play some slow music to encourage the children to move at a slower pace when first getting familiar with the *Clip Clop Cans*.

Talk about the distance to maintain between *Clip Clop Can* users. Practice looking ahead instead of down while walking so as not to bump into each other. Never try running, jumping or hopping on the *Clip Clop Cans*.

Make it Today for Pre-K Play   © Edupress

Further Activities

Older children are ready for more challenges as their confidence builds. After some degree of mastery is achieved, encourage further experimentation. Try standing on one can and lifting the other foot slightly off the ground. Try taking one or two steps backwards. Use directionality words and have the children move forward, backwards and sideways while on their *Clip Clop Cans*.

Set up a course for the children to walk through that provides some different challenges. Make curves and turns that they must manipulate through with their *Clip Clop Cans*.

Add an occasional obstacle along the way that they must maneuver around or step over. Use such items as cardboard boxes and flat tiles that pose no danger should a "Clip-Clopper" not negotiate the obstacle.

CLIP CLOP CANS

More Movement

Music   (See Resources, page 80.)

Slow and relaxing music can be found on **Movin'** by Hap Palmer. *Midnight Moon, Gentle Sea, and Enter Sunlight* are three good choices.

Older children may try a simplified rendition of the "Hokey Pokey "on their *Clip Clop Cans*. Sing the song together or play a version from **Kidding Around With Greg and Steve,** Youngheart Records, **All-Time Favorite Children's Games** by Georgiana Liccione Stewart or **All-Time Rhythm Favorites** by Jack Capon and Rosemary Hallum, Ph. D.

Chants

> *Clip clop I go on my cans all around*
> *By beautiful houses to the next town.*
> *I must be very careful as I move on by,*
> *To be sure I do not fall,*
> *For on the ground I will lie!*

When getting ready to put *Clip Clop Cans* away say the following chant:

> *You've clip-clopped here, you've clip-clopped there.*
> *And now it's time to rest your weary self.*
> *Move your cans along as you take care,*
> *So you can place them back upon the shelf.*

Game

You'll need, per team:
  • *Clip Clop Cans*   • 2 tennis balls   • 1 carpet remnant

Play this game with older children. Divide into teams. Mark a turn-around point with a carpet remnant approximately 18 feet from the starting line. The first child in line holds a *Clip Clop Can* in each hand. (Remove the plastic lid to enable children to grasp the open edge of the can.) Set a tennis ball on each can. At a signal, the first person in line moves as quickly as possible to the turn around point and back to the next person in line. If the tennis ball rolls of when moving, replace it and continue on. Vary with different kinds of balls.

CLIP CLOP CANS

Curriculum Integration

Math

Practice counting on your *Clip Clop Cans*. Invite several children to get on the *Clip Clop Cans*. While the class counts aloud together, the children on the *Clip Clop Cans* take a step for each number counted. Practice counting backwards, too. Move backwards on the *Clip Clop Cans!*

Snack

Send home a note a day prior to this activity, asking each child to bring in a snack food or drink that comes in a can. Compare the different cans by size, shape, color and weight. Find out if the cans need to be opened in different ways such as with a pop top or can opener. When everyone is hungry share a feast with the contents of the cans! Then set up a washing station to clean and dry all the cans together. Save the cans for the art project below.

Art

Use the empty cans left over from snack to construct a huge class sculpture. Allow the children to use their own creativity as they make their unique structure. Provide them with glue, scissors, construction paper scraps or any other odds and ends you might have in your room. Stack the cans in any order and angle. Have the glue gun ready (adult use only) to secure the cans in place.

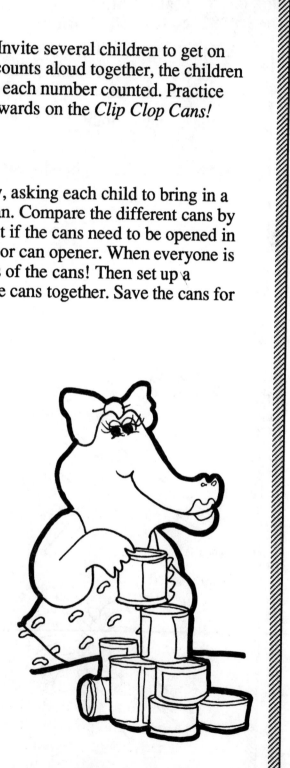

What to do with unused cans? Recycle them, of course! Turn them into pencil holders, make paint printings or dispose of them at a recycling center and do your part for the environment!

Materials Needed to Make One Swishy Streamer:

- Plastic tube used in golf club bags to separate clubs or small diameter wooden dowel
- Plastic table cloths in several different colors
- Sturdy scissors
- Sandpaper
- Masking tape
- Hand saw

"Swishy Streamers are short hand-held poles used to develop spatial awareness, unilateral and cross lateral movements."

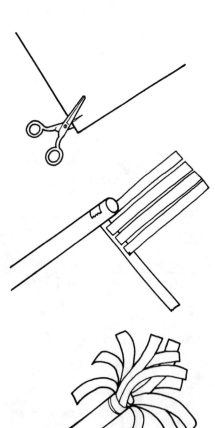

Assembling Directions:

1. Cut the table cloths into 1-inch (2.54 cm) wide strips approximately 18 inches (46 cm) in length. For younger children, decrease this length to 12 inches (32 cm).

2. Cut the golf club tube in half or the dowel into 12-inch (32 cm) lengths. Sand the ends to remove rough or sharp edges.

3. Cut a 12-inch (32 cm) strip of masking tape.

4. Attach 1 inch (2.54 cm) of the tape to the end of the tube or dowel. Leave most of the sticky side of the tape exposed.

5. One at a time, attach the table cloth strips on the masking tape as you wrap the tape around the tube or dowel. Colors may be varied.

6. Continue to wrap and add colored strips until the tape is completely wrapped around the dowel or tube. For fuller streamers, add more tape and plastic strips.

Make it Today for Pre-K Play   © Edupress

SWISHY STREAMERS

Motor Development Skills

- Cross-Lateral Movement
- Unilateral Movement
- Spatial Awareness
- Body Awareness

Safety Rules

- Be sure to allow enough room to swing the *Swishy Streamer* without hitting someone.
- Do not shake a *Swishy Streamer* in someone's face.
- Hold onto the *Swishy Streamer* tightly so that it will not fly out of your hand and hurt someone.

Teaching Tips

- ※ *Swishy Streamers* are appropriate for all ages . You may modify the length of the equipment and hand grip for different ages.

- ※ It is best to have enough *Swishy Streamers* for each child in the group.

- ※ If children are moving with the *Swishy Streamer* have them hold them high so that they will not step on the strips and pull them out.

- ※ Change hands frequently when using the *Swishy Streamer* so that one side of the body will not tire. It is also important to develop motor skills on both sides of the body.

- ※ You may want to make the *Swishy Streamer* in rainbow colors. You may also want some made with a single color strip attached to be used for color recognition activities.

SWISHY STREAMERS

Getting Started

Before handing out *Swishy Streamers*, give each child a "space of their own" to stand in so that children have plenty of room to freely move without hitting others with their *Swishy Streamer*. Practice the arm movements with an imaginary streamer. Swing the arms around the body. Make large and small arm circles. Wave the arm back and forth along the side and in front of the body. Repeat the movement with the other arm.

When distributing the *Swishy Streamer*, give it to the child so that he or she is able to grasp the handle and not the streamer end.

Encourage the children to hold the *Swishy Streamer* still until you are ready to use them. This can be accomplished by directing the children to place the streamers on their shoulder or to "freeze" in position.

Once the entire group has their *Swishy Streamer*, teach them a proper grip. The *Swishy Streamer* should be placed in the palm of their hand with their fingers wrapped around the end of the handle.

Allow the children time to experience the equipment for awhile. Then demonstrate other movements. Make a circle in front of the body. Swing the *Swishy Streamer* back and forth along the side of the body. Make a lasso above the head. Cast out like a fishing pole. Sweep side to side on the floor and "swoosh" behind the body. Have children duplicate the moves. They may need "hands-on" manipulation at first to master the movements.

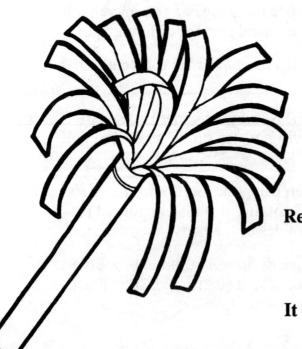

Remind children to change hands as they are using the streamers to avoid exhaustion of one side of the body or the other.

It should take several lessons with the streamers to introduce the many different movements.

Further Activities

Once the children have learned several different ways to move their *Swishy Streamer* you'll find you can easily relate the activity to a season, holiday or current theme.

During Autumn the *Swishy Streamer* can be falling leaves or a rake to gather the leaves in a pile. The *Swishy Streamer* becomes a flying bat at Halloween, a scurrying turkey at Thanksgiving or a flying sleigh at Christmas. During winter the *Swishy Streamer* can be snowflakes or snow shovels to get the snow off of the path. In the spring the *Swishy Streamer* can be a flower blooming, a bee buzzing or raindrops falling. In the summer time, go fishing with the *Swishy Streamer*.

Encourage children to think creatively to make up and relate movements to other different times of the year.

SWISHY STREAMERS

More Movement

Music   (See Resources, page 80)

Movin' by Hap Palmer provides a variety of instrumental songs to encourage create movement with the *Swishy Streamers*.

Learning With Circles and Sticks by Hap Palmer. *Circles Everywhere* and *Magic Stick* are also good songs for *Swishy Streamer* activities.

For curriculum integration, move *Swishy Streamers* to any holiday song.

Chants

Listen to the words and move the *Swishy Streamer*.

> *My streamers move high,*
> *And then they move low.*
> *I can also move them quite fast,*
> *And then very slow.*

> *My streamers swish left,*
> *And then to the right.*
> *If behind my back I place them,*
> *They go right out of sight!*

When it is time to end the *Swishy Streamer* activity remember to have the children walk with their streamers held high. This chant might serve as a reminder!

> *My streamers can touch the sky,*
> *I'll show you how as I fly by.*
> *The stars I shall reach for and hopefully catch,*
> *With my colorful streamers as I lay them to rest.*

SWISHY STREAMERS

Curriculum Integration

Literature

Incorporate the *Swishy Streamers* with weather or seasonal themes. These books will provide this integration.

Listen to the Rain by Bill Martin Jr. and John Archambault; Henry Holt and Company, 1988. A picture story about the sounds and feel of the rain.

The Wind Blew by Arthur Dorros; Thomas Y.Crowell 1989. A science-related book about the causes, feel and results of the wind.

Snack

Create an edible *Swishy Streamer*. Pull apart and eat a piece of string cheese.

Art

Create a *Swishy Streamer* to take home. Start with a plastic ring from a six-pack drink holder. Cut the ring apart into six circles.

Cut various color strips about 12 inches (30 cm) of crepe paper or plastic table cloth.

Let the children choose 3-5 colored strips. Wrap each one around the ring as shown. Tape or glue to hold in place.

To use, put your fingers through the ring's opening and close them to make a fist.

Science

Use the *Swishy Streamers* to teach children about rainbows. Have them make an arc in the air with the *Swishy Streamer* and talk about a rainbow's shape. Share the different colors seen in a rainbow. Do they have any of those colors in their *Swishy Streamer?* Paint a rainbow picture. Now hope for just the right day to see a rainbow in the sky!

© Edupress   Make it Today for Pre-K Play

7 LAUNCHING PADS

Materials Needed to Make One Launching Pad:

- 1/4- to 1/2-inch (1.25 cm) plywood
- 1- inch (2.54 cm) diameter dowel
- Circular saw
- Hand saw
- Hammer
- Sandpaper
- File
- Small nails
- Enamel paint, brush (optional)
- Permanent marker

"The Launching Pad is a simple catapult that is used to develop eye/hand and eye/foot coordination."

Assembling Directions:

1. Use the circular saw to cut the plywood into a 6 inch x 18 inch (15 cm x 45 cm) piece. Sand the cut edges.

2. Cut the dowel into a 5 1/2" (13 cm) length. File the dowel to get a flat edge on two opposite sides.

3. Nail one flat side of the dowel across the width and approximately 5 inches (12.5 cm) from one end of the plywood. Be sure the nails do not go through. (The dowel side is the bottom of the equipment.)

6. Paint the board a bright color (optional).

7. Draw a square on the top of the board opposite the dowel end to indicate bean bag placement.

8. Draw several stars on the top of the board, opposite the end with the square so children know where to stomp their foot.

Motor Development Skills

- Spatial Awareness
- Uniliateral Movement
- Eye/Hand Coordination
- Eye/Foot Coordination

Safety Rules

- Never run and jump onto the *Launching Pad*.
- Shoes should always be worn and children should be standing in the *Launching Pad* area.
- Space the *Launching Pad*s far enough apart to ensure toes are not stomped upon.

Teaching Tips

▨ Children love to run and jump onto the *Launching Pad* to see how high they can make the bean bag fly. This is not a safe move and may result in injury because the *Launching Pad* tends to slide out from under the child.

▨ Children also need to be reminded to move their *Launching Pad* back to where they started after each launch. The boards move with each stomp and can eventually wind up in an unsafe place.

▨ Using a larger diameter dowel with which to make the *Launching Pad* does not necessarily make this a better activity for children. Yes, the bean bag will fly higher but there will be more uncontrolled "launching" and less skill-building taking place.

LAUNCHING PADS

Getting Started

Begin by making sure the children fully understand the safety rules. Explain that only the feet should be used for stomping on the *Launching Pad*.

Before using the *Launching Pad* show the children how to stomp with the ball of the foot and their toes. Put on some "stomping" music and just practice for a while. Demonstrate and practice the difference between stomping with the toes versus stomping with the whole foot.

Next, demonstrate correct positioning of the *Launching Pad* in front of the body. Now they can practice stomping on the star end of the *Launching Pad*. Remind them again to use their toe area.

Show children the square that has been drawn at one end of the *Launching Pad*. Place a bean bag on the square. Demonstrate how the bean bag does not jump up when the whole foot is used. Now demonstrate a stomp with the upper part of the foot.

It's time for the children to experiment with the equipment. At first they will enjoy just seeing the bean bag being launched into the air and watching where it lands. After each launch, encourage them to try again by placing the bean bag back on the square and stomping on the star end of the *Launching Pad*. Younger children may not wish to go beyond this task.

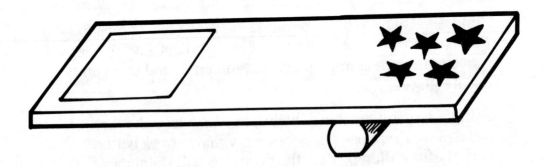

Once they have mastered launching the bean bag, children can go on to some more advanced skill building. Now upon launching, they should try to catch the bean bag in mid-air. This will take some practice as they develop the necessary motor skills.

Make it Today for Pre-K Play   © Edupress

Further Activities

Once the older children have had several attempts at using their launching pads encourage them to stomp and then catch the bean bag. Have them switch with a partner after they have caught the bean bag three times. As confidence builds have them catch with one hand. Next have them catch with their "other" hand.

Another fun activity is to try to launch and catch two bean bags. Let them keep increasing the number if they are capable. Have the children try to stomp on their board with first one foot and then the other.

Give a child five bean bags and let them launch them one at a time. Instruct the child that they are not to try to catch the bean bags. Let them see where they all land. Do they land in many different places?

A good cooperative partner activity is to let one child launch the bean bag while the other child tries to catch the it. Be sure to change roles half way through the activity.

LAUNCHING PADS

More Movement

Music   (See Resources, page 80.)

To get some experience in catching the bean bag use *Bean Bag Toss* and *Bean Bag Jungle* from **Me and My Bean Bag** by the Learning Station.

Also good is *Bean Bag Catch* from **Bean Bag Activities and Coordination Skills** by Georgina Liccione Stewart.

Chants

> *I saw a bean bag soaring high,*
> *I'm sure I just saw one fly by.*
> *If I reach out quickly maybe I can catch it,*
> *So my bean bag and I can rest and just sit.*

Sing to the tune of *Twinkle, Twinkle Little Star*:

> *Bean bag, bean bag, fly so high,*
> *Bean bag, bean bag, touch the sky.*
> *Stomp my toes and up you go,*
> *Where you land no one will know …*
> *Bean bag, bean bag, fly so high,*
> *Bean bag, bean bag, touch the sky.*

Game

Have the children form a large circle. Place a *Launching Pad* in the middle. Let each child find one small item in the room and take a turn trying to launch it using a *Launching Pad*. The items should be no bigger or heavier than the bean bags they used earlier. Give safety guidance, if necessary, when items are being chosen. Leave each item where it lands. Discuss the difference between heavier and lighter weight items. Do they move and land differently?

Curriculum Integration

Literature

__Cloudy With A Chance of Meatballs__ by Judy Barrett, Scholastic 1978.
Lots of food falls from the sky to feed the people of the town.

Snack

Have popcorn for a snack. Make sure you have more than you will need.
After snack take some of the leftover popcorn and let each child
launch a few pieces using a tongue depressor. Have them place the
tongue depressor at the edge of their table with half of it hanging over
the edge. Place the popcorn down on the end that is on the table.
Instruct them to hit the end hanging off of the table to see what
happens!

Counting

Use styrofoam packing pieces, bottle caps or other lightweight to reinforce
counting. Start by placing
one item on the *Launching
Pad* and launching it. Now
count together and place
two items on the
Launching Pad. Continue
counting and launching.

Science

Talk about how a rocket ship is
launched. Share pictures
of a rocket "take-off"
Practice counting
backwards together while
getting ready to launch a
bean bag.

8 CRISS CROSS CONES

Materials Needed to Make One Set of Criss-Cross Cones:

- 2 Orange safety/sport/traffic cones —18" (45 cm) to 24" (60 cm) height
- Plastic golf club separating tube (ask at the sporting goods store)
- 2 fishing weights (sized to fit through the cone's top opening yet heavy enough to anchor the rope)
- Ice pick   • Masking tape
- Nylon clothesline rope • Scissors

> **"Criss Cross Cones are simplified hurdles to cross over or under while developing lateral and locomotor skills."**

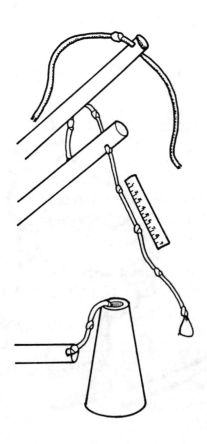

Assembling Directions:

1. Use the ice pick to poke a hole through both sides of each tube end. Thread a 24" (60 cm) to 30" (75 cm) length of rope through each hole. (Use a longer rope with the taller cone.)

2. Push the rope through just far enough to be able to tie several knots so that it will not slip back through the holes.

3. Cut off the excess rope and melt the ends together with a match. Repeat the process on the other end of the tube.

6. Tie a knot every six inches along the other end of the rope. The knots need to be spaced the same on each rope.

7. Tie a fishing weight on the end of each rope making sure the two ropes match exactly in length and knot placement.

Make it Today for Pre-K Play   © Edupres

CRISS-CROSS CONES

Motor Development Skills

- Cross-Lateral Movement
- Unilateral Movement
- Locomotor Skills
- Motor Planning

Safety Rules

- Children should never change the level of the crossbar.
- Crossbars should not be removed from the cones and swung in the air.
- When transporting crossbars, be sure to hold onto the weights to prevent them from swinging and hitting someone.

Teaching Tips

✎ Space the cones apart the distance of the plastic tube so that the fishing weights drop through the top hole of the cone.

✎ Placing the rope at the different knots that were tied in them enables you to change the level of the crossbar. Children can crawl under or cross over the *Criss Cross Cones*, increasing the number of skills that can be developed.

✎ *Criss Cross Cones* is a simple piece of equipment to create yet has so many uses. For example, two or three *Criss Cross Cones* can be spaced apart to create a hurdle track for children to run for gross motor development.

✎ Various heights of cones and lengths of tubes provide more opportunities to individualize your program. The plastic tubes can be cut in half to make a shorter crossing area. This creates a greater challenge for older children.

CRISS CROSS CONES

Getting Started

Before setting up the *Criss Cross Cones*, teach the children a few movements they will be doing when using them.

Begin with movements that will take them under the crossbar. Have them lie down on their stomach and move forward with a cross lateral "alligator" crawl. This is accomplished by moving both elbows forward and pulling followed by a knee crawl while still on the stomach. They need to work on keeping their bodies close to the ground. Younger children may have difficulty with cross lateral movements so encourage them to move unilaterally by using just one side of their body, elbow and knee pulling them forward at the same time. Challenge them to devise other ways to move forward while staying low to the ground. They can also practice moving backwards while on their stomachs.

Once the children are pretty confident with these "low-to-the-ground" movements, set up a course with the *Criss Cross Cones*. Having to negotiate under several sets of *Criss Cross Cones* brings a new element to the movement.

Next work on stepping over the crossbar. Step forward then backward. Children should be taught to let the crossbar fall with them should they hit it or get caught in it when moving. Vary the height of the crossbar by moving the rope to a different knot. Once stepping has been mastered, practice hopping and jumping over the crossbar at different heights.

Set up several sets of *Criss Cross Cones* in a course in which children must step over the crossbar. They can move forward, backwards or sideways through the course.

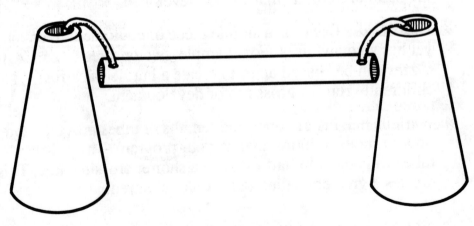

Further Activities

Set up a challenging course of *Criss Cross Cones* for older children that requires them to go over and under the cones using all the movements they have practiced. They should be encouraged to alternate feet when stepping or hopping over to increase laterality.

A picture card can be placed at each set of *Criss Cross Cones* that shows children the movement they are to perform there. Pictures can also relate to a holiday, seasonal or other curriculum theme. For example, during Easter or spring celebrations, a picture of a bunny would tell the child to jump over the *Criss Cross Cones*, an egg would mean roll under and a basket would mean step over the crossbar. Introduce the pictures and practice their corresponding movements to the children in advance.

Have the children continue the designated movement as they travel from one *Criss Cross Cone* to the next in the course. There they will see a new picture and proceed with a new movement.

Younger children should be able to follow a simple picture direction. They may find more success, however, walking from one *Criss Cross Cone* set to another rather than trying to continue the movement in the picture. Younger children might also do better with an actual picture of the skill required rather than a thematic picture.

CRISS CROSS CONES

More Movement

Music   (See Resources, page 80.)

Tummy Tango from **Kids in Motion** by Greg and Steve, Youngheart Records is a song about moving all different ways while down on your stomach. There are great movements to do under the *Criss Cross Cones*.

Children of all ages should enjoy doing *Zippity Doo Dah* through a *Criss Cross Cones* course. Check **Good Morning Exercises for Kids** by Georgiana Stewart for a good version of this standard tune.

Chants

> *I criss cross my arms,*
> *I criss cross my feet.*
> *A knot I will forever be.*

> *Uncross those arms,*
> *Uncross those feet.*
> *Or a knot you shall forever be,*

> *Under, Over, Here we go.*
> *Under, Over, Take it slow.*
> *On your tummy,*
> *slither and crawl.*
> *On your tummy,*
> *have a ball.*
> *Hop and Jump,*
> *Twist and turn.*
> *Hop and Jump,*
> *It's fun to learn!*

Game

Thirty Second Challenge from **Learning Basic Skills Through Music Volume V** by Hap Palmer is a good source for games when reinforcing a new concept such as number recognition. Cards with simple pictures depicting the concept you wish to review could be placed at an end of a course that involves going over and under the crossbars of the *Criss Cross Cones*.

Curriculum Integration

Literature

Stories about crawling things go along with all of the crawling children do under the crossbars.

The Greedy Python by Richard Buckley, Scholastic Inc. 1985. This is a playful story about a very hungry python.

Crictor by Tomi Underer, Scholastic Book Services 1958. Crictor is a snake who has many fun and helpful experiences with his owner.

Snack

To extend the theme of crawling things, give each child a ball of cookie dough. Let them shape the ball into a crawling cookie creature! Bake and eat!

Art

Follow the recipe for making baker's dough with the children. From the dough they can create their own crawly creature to take home!

You'll need:
- 2 cups flour
- 2 cups salt
- 1 cup water
- 1 cup oil

Mix together, shape and bake at 325 degrees until dough feels dry and hard.

Add food coloring to the recipe to make dough in different colors. Or, you can finish the hardened dough creatures with tempera paint.

Science

Learn about jumping, hopping and slithering animals. Find out about kangaroos and snakes. Do monkeys jump? Do elephants hop? How do animals move?

BEANY BAGS

Materials Needed to Make One Beany Bag:

- Colorful, sturdy fabric scraps (Check with a local upholsterer)
- Dried beans
- Scoop or funnel
- Sewing machine
- Fabric scissors

> "Beany Bags are throwing toys that build a large variety of motor development skills."

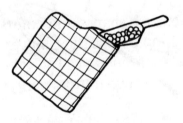

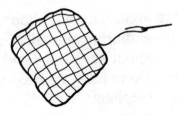

Assembling Directions:

1. Cut two 6-inch square (15 cm) fabric pieces.

2. With wrong sides together, sew three sides and half of the fourth side of the fabric together.

3. Double-stitch the seams for extra reinforcement.

4. Turn the pouch right-side-out.

5. Use the funnel or scoop to help fill the pouch about 3/4 full with dried beans.

4. Sew the opening closed. Double stitch for reinforcement.

Make it Today for Pre-K Play   © Edupress

Motor Development Skills

- Cross-Lateral Movement
- Laterality
- Eye/Hand Coordination
- Body Awareness

Safety Rules

- Never throw a *Beany Bag* at another person.
- If a *Beany Bag* has a hole in it, tell an adult immediately.
- If beans should fall out of the bag, pick them up and throw them away.
- Never put any beans in your mouth.

Teaching Tips

※ You will find you use the *Beany Bags* frequently in a variety of classroom programs. When they get dirty simply sew clean fabric over the old to give the *Beany Bag* new life!

※ *Beany Bags* can be made in different sizes, shapes and colors. The more colorful the *Beany Bag* the more appealing it is to use! You can also use *Beany Bags* as manipulatives for reinforcing shape, categorizing and color recognition.

※ It is a good idea to have at least one *Beany Bag* for every child in your class. More than one per child may be necessary for some activities.

※ Purchase a colorful bucket at a hardware store for *Beany Bag* storage. Paint bright lettering on the outside of the bucket to indicate its contents. Transporting the *Beany Bags* will be easier ... and so will clean-up!

BEANY BAGS

Getting Started

Children will want to touch and explore the *Beany Bag* the first time you hand them out. Take advantage of this opportunity for a "sense" exploration experience. Have the children close their eyes and squeeze the bag. Ask them if they can guess what is inside. Try smelling and squeezing the bag some more for clues. Have some dried beans on hand to share after the guessing game. This is also a good time to discuss safety rules relating to the *Beany Bags*.

Next space the children around the room so they have plenty of room to move their arms and bodies freely. You may want to head outside if indoor space is limited.

Encourage the children to try different ways of moving their bean bags while they sit and stand. Hold the bag in one hand, then the other. Make shapes in the air while holding the bag in the hand.

Try some balancing activities. Balance the *Beany Bag* on the back of the hand, in the palm of the hand, on a shoulder or top of the head. Sit cross-legged and balance the *Beany Bag* on each knee.

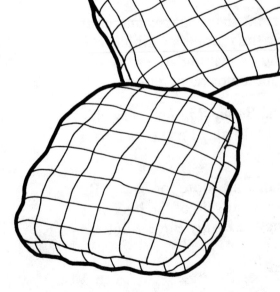

Now attempt some eye/hand coordination movements. Try tossing the *Beany Bag* a few inches (or centimeters) into the air and catching it with the same hand. As success is achieved, the height of the throw can be increased.

The *Beany Bag* can also be tossed from one hand to another. Increase the height of the toss and distance apart of the hands as skill develops.

Make it Today for Pre-K Play   © Edupress

Further Activities

All children can review directionality skills by placing the *Beany Bag* over, under or beside their body.

Beany Bags can be used to balance on a head or shoulder while walking forward or backwards. Older children can be further challenged by moving with the *Beany Bag* on a balance beam.

Children can throw the *Beany Bag* back and forth with a partner. Older children can try to catch with a left hand or right hand, above their bodies, beside their bodies or in other imaginative ways.

Use the *Beany Bag* to develop locomotor skills, too. The children can place their *Beany Bag* on the ground in front of them and jump, hop or leap over it. They can skip or gallop in a circle around it. Then ask older children to move their body so the *Beany Bag* is in front of them, behind them and beside them. Directionality terms such as left and right can also be used.

BEANY BAGS

More Movement

Music

There are many wonderful albums that are entirely for bean bag activities. Two are especially good for early childhood. (See Resources, page 80.)

Me and My Bean Bag by the Learning Station.

Bean Bag Activities & Coordination Skills by Georgiana Liccione Stewart.

Chants

> *I throw my Beany Bag way up high,*
> *I hope it will sail across the deep blue sea.*
> *But no matter what I do it wants to fly,*
> *Right back into my arms to be with me.*

To end a *Beany Bag* activity say the following chant:

> *Beany Bags are fun to toss all around town,*
> *Up and down and all about my Beany Bag and I go.*
> *Now it is time to stop and rest but do not make a frown,*
> *For we had fun whereever we went whether it was high or low.*

Game

You'll need:
- one bean bag sewn on three sides but not filled
- dried beans

Show children a filled *Beany Bag*. Ask them to guess how many beans they think it will take to fill the *Beany Bag*. After everyone has guessed, fill the bag, counting as you fill. How close were the children's guesses to the actual amount?

Curriculum Integration

Science

You'll need
- beans
- small bowl
- scotch tape
- clear plastic cups, two per child
- cotton balls
- water

Conduct a bean-sprouting experiment. Soak some beans overnight in a bowl of water. The next day, give each child two plastic cups and a cotton ball. Place one soaked bean into a cup. Put a wet cotton ball on top of the bean. Invert the second cup over the first. Seal the cups together with scotch tape. Place in a sunny location. Wait and observe for several days!

Literature

Connect literature with science.

Fruit by Gallimard Jeunesse and Pascale de Bourgoing, Scholastic Inc. 1989. This book features cross-section transfer pictures of fruits and seeds.

The Reason for a Flower by Ruth Heller, Grosset & Dunlap 1983. Illustrations show *the reason for a flower*.

Snack

Cook up some beany recipes. Try a three-bean salad, crock pot bean soup or a refried bean burrito.

Art

You'll need:
- many kinds of dried beans
- white glue
- sturdy cardboard

Give each child an assortment of beans to glue in a design a piece of cardboard.

SIT-DOWN SCOOTERS

10

Materials Needed to Make One Sit-Down Scooter:

- 3/4-inch (2 cm) plywood
- Four caster wheels with screws
- Thick carpet remnant
- Varnish and paint brush
- Saw
- Carpet knife
- Sandpaper
- Screwdriver
- Strong glue
- One cupboard handle

> "A Sit-Down Scooter is a rolling seat that develops locomotor skills, unilateral and bilateral movements."

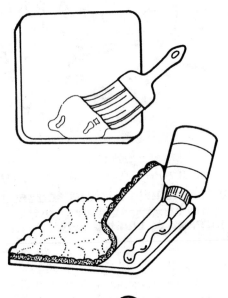

Assembling Directions:

1. Cut the plywood into a 16-inch (40 cm) square. Slightly round the corners.

2. Sand the board and corners to a smooth finish.

3. Varnish the edges and one side of the board.

4. Cut a carpet square the same size as the plywood square.

5. Glue the carpet square to the unfinished side of the board.

6. Screw the four casters to each corner of the varnished side of the board.

7. Attach the cupboard handle to one side of the bottom of the scooter for carrying purposes.

SIT-DOWN SCOOTERS

Motor Development Skills

- Unilateral Movement
- Bilateral Movement
- Directionality
- Locomotor Skills
- Tactile Awareness

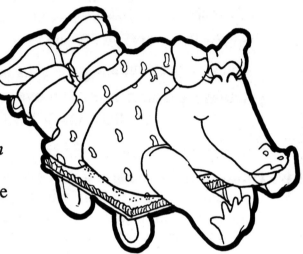

Safety Rules

- Never run and land on the *Sit-Down Scooter*.
- Do not run into a friend while on the *Sit-Down Scooter*.
- Watch out for other people's hands and feet while on the *Sit-Down Scooter*. Keep movement in control.

Teaching Tips

✎ This equipment is appropriate for all ages. Beginners should always keep their stomachs on the *Sit-Down Scooter*.

✎ Try to set aside an area of the playground that is for *Sit-Down Scooter* use during outdoor recess and breaks. Children love this equipment and will want to use it often.

✎ Because children of all ages are interested in the actions they see (or have experienced) on roller blades, skates or skateboards, they may want to try these same kinds of things on their *Sit-Down Scooter*. Explain to the children the dangers of duplicating these actions. A *Sit-Down Scooter* reacts differently than other "rolling" equipment and accidents can easily happen.

✎ Allow plenty of space so that each child has room to freely move the *Sit-Down Scooter* without bumping into others.

SIT-DOWN SCOOTERS

Getting Started

Before allowing children to use the *Sit-Down Scooters*, be sure they fully understand the safety rules. It is natural for them to want to stand on the *Sit-Down Scooter* like on a skateboard or run and land on them. No matter the level of mastery or confidence, do not allow either of these activities.

Once children understand the rules, have them lie on the floor on their stomach. Ask them to try to move using only their arms and feet. Once they are able to do this movement they should be ready to try the *Sit-Down Scooter* .

Have children start on the *Sit-Down Scooter* by placing their stomach on the carpeted side, then pulling with their hands and pushing off with their feet. Younger children will find this position to be the most successful. They may take awhile before progressing to other positions.

As children gain confidence, let them sit on the *Sit-Down Scooters* and use only their feet to move. Next they can kneel on the *Sit-Down Scooters*, lean and use their hands and arms to propel them.

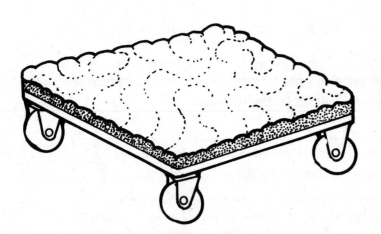

Older children, or those who master preceding movements, may try lying on their back or sides and creating their own way to make the *Sit-Down Scooters* move. As they gain more freedom, talk about the motions involved in achieving movement on the *Sit-Down Scooter* and the additional safety rules they need to follow.

A final challenge could be to have a child stretch their body out on the floor, stomach touching. Place only the feet on the *Sit-Down Scooter*. Try walking with the hands while keeping the arms very straight.

Further Activities

Plan some races for older children. Establish teams with one *Sit-Down Scooter* for each team. Vary the relay race by incorporating some of the positions suggested in **Getting Started**. Encourage students to contribute to the ideas for positions to use on the *Sit-Down Scooter* during the races.

Make a course in which children have to maneuver their *Sit-Down Scooter* under or around Criss-Cross Cones (see page 50). Again, experiment with various body positions on the *Sit-Down Scooter* while moving through the course or path.

Sit-Down Scooters provide a fun and varied way to move from one activity or station to another in an obstacle course.

Build upper body agility by having a child hold onto a long rope while lying on their stomach on the *Sit-Down Scooter*. An adult holds onto the other end of the rope and extends it to its fullest, stretched position. The child on the *Sit-Down Scooter* then uses a hand-over-hand movement to get to the adult at the other end.

SIT-DOWN SCOOTERS

More Movement

Music

While on the *Sit-Down Scooter* it is fun to do a "scooter"version of the "Hokey Pokey." The same songs suggested in Clip-Clop Cans, (see page 36), would be appropriate . Children enjoy repetition of familiar games and songs. They become more active participants.

Switch On the Music from **Rhythms on Parade** by Hap Palmer (see Resources, page 80) is also good music to accompany *Sit-Down Scooter* activities.

Chants

> *My scooter takes me wherever I want to go,*
> *Up and down hills or to see where the river flows.*
> *Without my friend the scooter*
> *I could never see,*
> *Something as beautiful*
> *As a forest full of trees.*

End a *Sit-Down Scooter* activity with this chant.

> *Scoot here, scoot there, we've scooted everywhere!*
> *We've even used our scooter just like a chair!*
> *My Sit-Upon Scooter is tired and so am I.*
> *We're both going to rest now*
> *Where we can find a place to lie.*

Creative Movement

Ask children to pretend to move like different vehicles such as an airplane, car, spaceship or train while on their *Sit-Down Scooter*. They can simulate the sounds the vehicles make, too. Try to guess what each child is pretending to be.

66

SIT-DOWN SCOOTERS

Curriculum Integration

Social Studies

Incorporate *Sit-Down Scooters* into a study of transportation, wheels or things that "go".

Connect with literature:

> *On the Go* by Ann Morris; Scholastic Inc. 1990. Photographic book about methods of transportation all over the world.

> *Mr. Little's Noisy Truck* by Richard Fowler; Grosset & Dunlap, 1989. A book about the adventures of a noisy delivery truck.

Snack

Make wheel-shaped macaroni and cheese. Cook macaroni as directed. Add a can of cheddar cheese soup and 1/2 can milk. Mix together and heat.

Art

Movement Painting:

Dip the wheels of plastic cars in tempera paint. "Drive" the cars over paper to make a design.

Wheel Collage:

Dye wheel-shaped macaroni in a mixture of rubbing alcohol and a few drops of food coloring. Toss with a spoon until the desired color is achieved. Drain and dry on paper toweling.

Glue different color wheels on sturdy paper to create a collage. Use markers or crayons to complete the picture.

LUMMI STICKS

11

Materials Needed to Make One Pair of Lummi Sticks:

- 2 feet (62 cm) of 3/4" - 1" (2.54 cm) diameter wood dowel (PVC pipe may be substituted)
- Small hand saw
- Sandpaper
- Enamel paint (optional)
- Colored plastic tape (optional)

"Lummi Sticks are rhythm instruments that develop the midline, lateral, unilateral and bilateral movements."

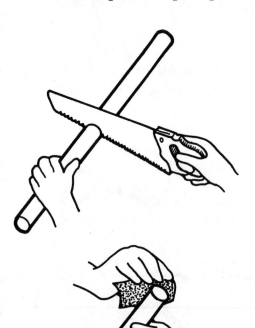

Assembling Directions:

1. Use the hand saw to cut the PVC (or wood dowel) into two, one-foot (30 cm) lengths.

2. Sand the cut ends until smooth.

3. Paint the dowels with enamel paint in a bright color. Vary the color of the pairs if making more than one.

4. If using PVC pipe, cover the cut ends with colored plastic tape. Paint will not adhere properly to PVC pipe. Again, vary the color of tape on each pair of *Lummi Sticks* if you are making more that one set.

LUMMI STICKS

Motor Development Skills

- Midline
- Laterality
- Unilateral Movement
- Bilateral Movement

Safety Rules

- Never use your *Lummi Sticks* to hit another person.
- Be sure you have room to move the *Lummi Sticks* without making contact with anyone around you.
- Hold your *Lummi Sticks* correctly to avoid hitting your own fingers.

Teaching Tips

※ *Lummi Sticks* are fun and serve a wonderful purpose however they can easily turn into a negative experience if you do not establish ground rules right from the start.

※ Store the *Lummi Sticks* upright in a bucket.

※ Bucket storage facilitates handing out the equipment. The children pass the bucket and take out a set of *Lummi Sticks* when the bucket reaches them. Challenge them to hold their *Lummi Sticks* in a pre-established position until everyone has chosen theirs. Select a position that reinforces current study focus. Otherwise you will have uncontrolled tapping. For example, "Hold your *Lummi Sticks* between your knees." (Body parts). "Put your *Lummi Sticks* on the ground behind you." (Directionality)

LUMMI STICKS

Getting Started

Have the children sit cross-legged on the ground. Pass the *Lummi Stick* bucket. (See **Teaching Tips**). Ask each child to take a pair of *Lummi Sticks* out of the bucket and set them on the ground in front of them.

Begin by learning how to hold the *Lummi Sticks* correctly. Tell the children to pick them up, one in each hand, by wrapping their fingers around the stick. Next have them rest one stick on each knee. Their thumbs should be on the top. Show them how to slide their hands down the sticks so that the fist they have made around the stick is touching their knee. The palms of their hands should be about 1-inch (2.54 cm) from the end of the stick.

Practice picking up and putting down the *Lummi Sticks* until the holding position is mastered and comfortable for each child.

One of the first activities to do with the *Lummi Sticks* is to use them as pointers for different body parts. Younger children can use one stick to point to the different body parts you name. The other stick should be resting on the ground in front of them. Older children can do the same activity with their eyes closed. This not only reinforces body awareness but also makes children more aware of the space required to move the *Lummi Sticks* around them.

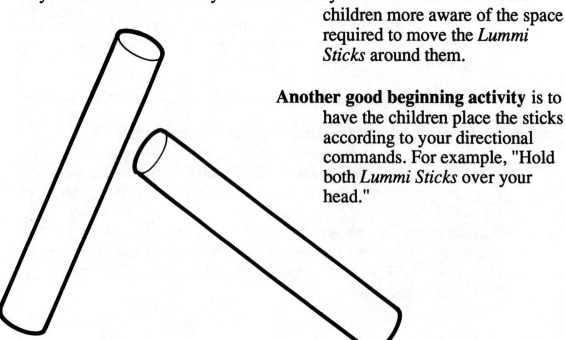

Another good beginning activity is to have the children place the sticks according to your directional commands. For example, "Hold both *Lummi Sticks* over your head."

70

Further Activities

As the children become familiar with the *Lummi Sticks*, introduce some
music. Choose from the suggestions on the following page.

Form the class into a large circle with plenty of room between each child.
Encourage the children to create their own movements with the
Lummi Sticks while listening to music.

Marching and tapping to the beat is another fun *Lummi Stick* activity. Tap
the sticks together or provide empty shoe boxes to serve as "drums"
on which to tap the *Lummi Sticks* .

Develop auditory memory by asking the children to repeat a tapped pattern.

Reinforce counting by tapping a specified number of times.

LUMMI STICKS

More Movement

Music   (See Resources, page 80.)

Rhythms on Parade by Hap Palmer has three good *Lummi Stick* selections.

• *Woodpecker* plays a rhythm the children can follow by tapping their *Lummi Sticks*. Some of the rhythms in this selection are fast and long so this is a better activity for older children.

• *Tap Your Sticks* develops left and right directionality. Have younger children tap side to side rather than than right and left.

• *Roller Coaster* encourages creative movement. Children can rub the *Lummi Sticks* together, move them up and down, tap high in the air or down on the ground. They can move the *Lummi Sticks* up and down and fast and slow the way a roller coaster moves. This song is not specifically suggested for *Lummi Sticks* and will fit other area of your program as well.

Simplified Lummi Stick Activities by Laura Johnson, is specifically for use with the *Lummi Sticks*. One side has words while the other side is instrumental. If younger children find the words too difficult to follow, use the instrumental side and make up your own movements.

Chants

> *My sticks can hammer,*
> *My sticks can pound.*
> *Where the noise they make*
>   *is coming from,*
> *Cannot always be found.*

> *I can tap my sticks up high,*
> *And then I tap them very low.*
> *And when I am all through my*
>   *sticks know to lay,*
> *All in a row.*

Game

Play a shape game that encourages cooperative learning. Place the children in small groups. Ask them to make a large shape such as a square or a rectangle using all of their *Lummi Sticks*.

Make it Today for Pre-K Play   © Edupress

Curriculum Integration

Literature

The Tree by Gallimard Jeunesse and Pascale de Bourgoing; Scholastic Inc. 1989. Transparencies let you see inside the leaves, seeds, and branches of a tree. Find the stick shapes in the tree parts.

The Very Quiet Cricket by Eric Carle; Scholastic Book Club Edition, 1990. Go on an adventure with a cricket and compare the opposite sounds of quiet and tapping.

Snack

Munch on pretzel sticks for snack! Compare the shape to the *Lummi Sticks*.

Color Recognition

If you did not paint or put different color tape on the *Lummi Sticks* when they were made, tape a piece of colored construction paper around each stick for this skill-building activity. Pass out all the *Lummi Sticks* . Listen to music and tap together by color. "All those who have a blue *Lummi Stick*, tap it now."

Science/Environment

Go on a nature walk. Let the children pick up any sticks they find on the ground. This might include twigs, sticks, popsicle sticks and toothpicks.

Back in the classroom divide a poster board in half. Write **Good** on one half and **Bad** on the other. Together, divide the items into natural items and things that hurt our environment Glue them to the corresponding poster half. Display the poster in the classroom for all to share.

JUMPING BEAN BOX

Materials Needed to Make One Jumping Bean Box:

- Sheet of 3/4-inch (2 cm) plywood
- Wood glue   • Saw
- 2 handles   • Hammer, nails
- Screwdriver   • Sandpaper
- Carpet knife   • Varnish, paint brush
- 2 Angle iron loops and hooks
- Thick indoor/outdoor carpeting

"A Jumping Bean Box is a platform with a ramp attached that is used to develop motor planning and body awareness."

Assembling Directions:

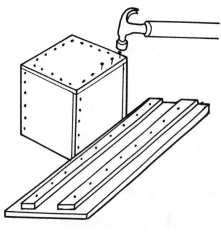

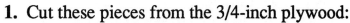

1. Cut these pieces from the 3/4-inch plywood:
   - One 16 " (40 cm) square
   - Four 16"x 18" (40 cm x 45cm) rectangles
   - One 68" x 16" (154 cm x 40 cm) rectangle
   - Two 2" x 60" (5 cm x 150 cm) rectangles

2. Sand all pieces. Glue, then nail, the 16"x 18" sides to the square top to create a five-sided box. Cut carpet to fit the box top and rectangle ramp. Glue in place. Varnish exposed wood.

3. On the ramp's varnished side, nail the 2"x 60" reinforcing strips 2" (5 cm) from the edge.

4. On one side of the box, attach the iron loops 3/4" (2 cm) from the top and 12"(30 cm) apart. On one end of the unvarnished side of the ramp, screw the angle iron hooks 12" apart . They must match up with the loops on the side of the box. There should be no gap between the top of the box and the ramp when connected.

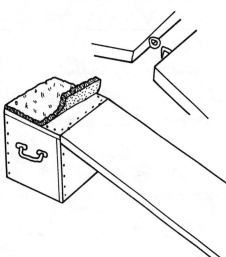

5. Screw the two handles on opposite sides of the box for carrying purposes.

74

JUMPING BEAN BOX

Motor Development Skills

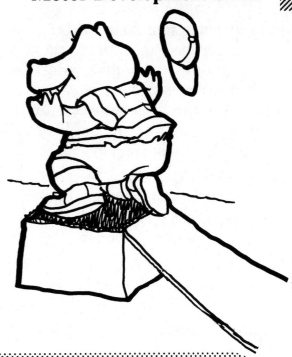

- Cross-Lateral Movement
- Bilateral Movement
- Motor Planning
- Body Awareness

Safety Rules

- Do not climb on or jump off the *Jumping Bean Box* without directions from an adult.
- Always jump and land exactly as you have been shown.
- Never push or pull a friend on or off the *Jumping Bean Box*.
- Only one person should be on the *Jumping Bean Box* at a time.

Teaching Tips

✎ One *Jumping Bean Box* should be sufficient for a classroom. This activity needs close supervision. More than one *Jumping Bean Box* would require additional adult supervision.

✎ A *Jumping Bean Box* should not be introduced until children have learned how to jump and land on two feet at the same time.

✎ Children should also have plenty of exposure to the *Clip Clop Cans* and balance beam prior to using the *Jumping Bean Box*.

✎ A mat or padded carpet remnant should always be placed at the base of the *Jumping Bean Box* to absorb some of the impact when the children land.

✎ Be sure children know that toes should be at the edge of the platform before jumping to ensure a landing safely away from the *Jumping Bean Box*.

JUMPING BEAN BOX

Getting Started

Before learning to use the *Jumping Bean Box*, practice lots of jumping. Show children how to jump up and land squarely on two feet. Be sure they learn to absorb some of the impact of a jump by landing on slightly bent knees rather than straight legs. Also practice trying to fall forward rather than backwards on an unsuccessful landing. Encourage them not to get silly and fall forward on purpose. They will soon begin to feel the proper weight distribution on a jump.

Once jumping skills have been mastered, introduce the children to jumping off something that has some height. With assistance, try standing on the balance beam and jumping off. The *Jumping Bean Box* is 18 inches (45 cm) high so you will want to work gradually to this height.

Now it's time to share the *Jumping Bean Box*. Talk about what it looks like with the children. You should get responses like a slide or a square. Demonstrate the use of the ramp.

To begin, have the children walk up the ramp to the top of the box, stop at the top and plant their feet as if ready to jump. They may want you to hold their hand when first trying. When they appear ready, encourage them to jump. During their first attempts it is best if an adult is standing by the child who is jumping. Some children will need encouragement to make the jump. Hold their hand, or both hands if necessary to help them build up some courage! Most likely not every child will want to attempt this activity.

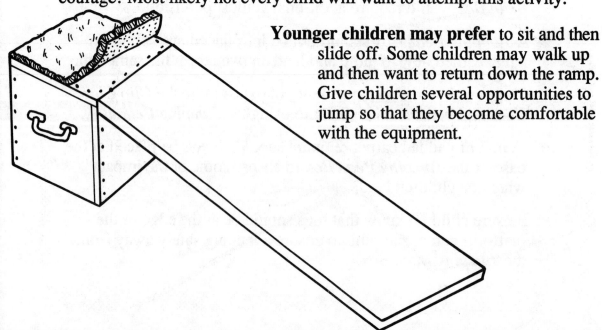

Younger children may prefer to sit and then slide off. Some children may walk up and then want to return down the ramp. Give children several opportunities to jump so that they become comfortable with the equipment.

Make it Today for Pre-K Play   © Edupress

JUMPING BEAN BOX

Further Activities

Once children are comfortable jumping off the *Jumping Bean Box*, suggest different ways to go up the ramp. Try crawling forward or backwards or stepping and sliding sideways. Jump from the box in different ways as well. Jump from a sideways position, spin in the air before landing or jump and land on feet and hands in a squatting position.

Older children can run up the ramp, plant their feet and jump. They also can land in a circle outlined in tape on the ground and then continue to jump through a circle pattern.

A further challenge for the children can be to jump and clap their hands two or three times before landing. If you are working on right or left directionality, have the children make a quarter turn in the air so they are facing either right or left upon landing. Once on the ground children can continue to jump around following your directions.

As confidence builds, let them try jumping off the *Jumping Bean Box* backwards. If a coordination ladder is available, try using that in place of the ramp in order to get on the *Jumping Bean Box*.

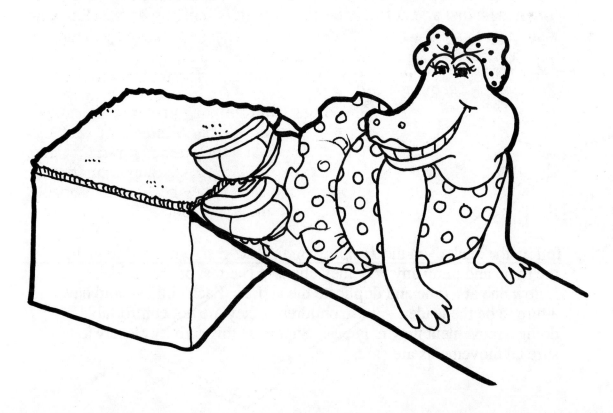

JUMPING BEAN BOX

More Movement

Music   (See Resources, page 80.)

It's Just Fun from **Feelin' Free** by Hap Palmer is a good song to act out as the
   children are waiting their turn on the *Jumping Bean Box.*

Listen and Move from **We All Live Together, Volume 2** by Greg and Steve,
   Youngheart Records is fun to follow as children move from the top of the
   Jumping Bean Box. The rest of the class can be doing the movements
   while waiting for their turn.

Chants

> *You can climb to the sky,*
> *Then you take off and you fly.*
> *You sail through the air,*
> *And hope that you land at a fair!*
>
> *The wind blows you down,*
> *Your face has a frown.*
> *For you're not at the fair,*
> *You just landed by my chair!*

> *Jump, jump, jump.*
> *Jump, jump, jump.*
> *Isn't that easy for you?*
>
> *Jump and clap.*
> *Jump and clap.*
> *Can you do these two?*
>
> *Jump, clap, giggle.*
> *Jump, clap, giggle.*
> *Isn't that fun to do?*

Game

Play "follow the leader" on the *Jumping Bean Box.* Ask one child to go up
   the ramp and jump any way they choose. The rest of the children
   follow one at a time and duplicate the actions. Each child should have
   a turn to be the leader. Assure children if they are not comfortable
   doing a movement they may pass. Supervise this activity closely to be
   sure all movements are safe.

78

Curriculum Integration

Literature

Read a story about a jumping animal. *Katy No-Pocket* by Emmy Payne, Houghton Mifflin, 1944, is about a mother kangaroo who cannot jump with her baby because she has no pocket.

Art

After having read *Katy No-Pocket* to the class the children will know how important the pocket was to Katy and what her solution was. Give each child a construction paper pocket. Tell them they are to create a magic pocket. Color and cut a picture of something to glue on the magic pocket.

Tape the pocket to their shirt or blouse. Encourage them to tell about the contents of their pocket.

Snack

Make some popcorn and watch it jump, pop and land like the children did on the *Jumping Bean Box*. Take a turn being a popping kernel of corn on the *Jumping Bean Box* then enjoy your snack!

Science

Ask the children to suggest an animal name. Have an animal book handy for the children to look through for ideas. Try jumping off the *Jumping Bean Box* in a way they think that animal might jump. An elephant might land with a loud thud. A snake might slither in the air. A bird might flap its wings. Think creatively and learn about animals, too!

RESOURCES

Additional Motor Development Equipment:
- Chinese Jump Ropes
- Hula Hoops
- Parachute
- Jump Ropes
- Playground Balls

Equipment to Add as the Budget Allows
- Coordination Ladder
- Geometric Shapes
- Balance Beam
- Scooter Boards
- Jump Box
- Rebound Nets

Books

Easy Games for Early Learners **Wendy Loreen**, Edupress, 1993.

The Joy of Music In Early Childhood **Dr. Sandra Curtis**, Teachers College Press.

The Outrageous Outdoor Games Book **Bob Gregson**, Fearon Teaching Aids, 1984.

Perceptual-Motor Lesson Plans Level-1 **Jack Capon**, Front Row, 1975.

Theme Days for Younger Years **Joyce Hamman**, Edupress, 1993.

Music

All-Time Favorite Children's Games **Georgiana Liccione Stewart** KIM 9068

All-Time Rhythm Favorites **Jack Capon and Rosemary Hallum, Ph.D.** AR 630

Bean Bag Activities and Coordination Skills **Georgiana Liccione Stewart** KIM 7055

Easy Does It **Hap Palmer** AR 581

Feelin' Free **Hap Palmer** AR 517

Good Morning Exercises for Kids **Georgiana Liccione Stewart** KIM 9098

Kidding Around with Greg and Steve, **Youngheart Records** CTP 007

Kids In Motion **Greg and Steve, Youngheart Records** CTP 008

Learning Basic Skills Through Music **Hap Palmer** AR 514

Learning Through Movement and Song, Volume 1 **Sheri Senter**
  National Pediatric Support Services

Learning with Circles and Sticks **Hap Palmer** AR 585

Me and My Bean Bag **The Learning Station** KIM 9111

Movin' **Hap Palmer** AR 546

Rhythms on Parade **Hap Palmer** AR 633

Songs About Me **Kimbo** KIM 70223

We All Live Together, Volume 2 **Greg and Steve, Youngheart Records** CTP 002